BIG
BEASTS

Komodo
Dragon

Stephanie Turnbull

Published by Smart Apple Media,
an imprint of Black Rabbit Books
P.O. Box 3263, Mankato, Minnesota, 56002
www.blackrabbitbooks.com

Designed by Hel James
Edited by Mary-Jane Wilkins

Cataloging-in-Publication Data is available
from the Library of Congress

ISBN 978-1-62588-200-4

Photo acknowledgements
l = left, r = right, t = top, b = bottom
title page Ekaterina V. Borisova/Shutterstock; page 3
Jose Bergadá; 4 MikeLane45; 5 Jo Ann Hill/all Thinkstock;
6 photo_journey/Shutterstock; 7 telnyawka; 8 Daniel Padavona/
both Thinkstock; 9 Ethan Daniels; 10 Patrick Rolands; 11 Norma
Cornes; 12 David Evison; 13 dean bertoncelj; 14, 15 Sergey
Uryadnikov/all Shutterstock; 16 Philip Stubbs/Thinkstock;
17 kkaplin/Shutterstock; 18 Paul Robinson/Thinkstock;
19 Stephen Belcher/Minden Pictures/FLPA; 20 ©Michael Pitts/
naturepl.com; 21 Colette3/Shutterstock; 22b kkaplin,
t RUSOTURISTO; 23 Pius Lee/all Shutterstock
Cover Levent Konuk/Shutterstock

Printed in China

DAD0059
032014
9 8 7 6 5 4 3 2 1

Contents

Killer Lizards 4

Living Wild 6

Sunbathing 8

On the Hunt 10

Attack! 12

Greedy Eaters 14

Deadly Bites 16

Fierce Fights 18

Climbing Babies 20

BIG Facts 22

Useful Words 24

Index 24

Komodo dragons are
enormous!

Killer Lizards

Komodo dragons are the biggest,
heaviest lizards on Earth.

They are fierce, terrifying meat-eaters.

Komodos are covered in hard, bumpy scales.

Their huge, muscular tail is as long as their body.

Living Wild

Wild Komodo dragons live on only five islands in Indonesia. Scientists didn't even know they existed until about 100 years ago.

Komodos live alone,
prowling through
tropical rainforests
and dry grasslands.

They may swim from
one island to another.

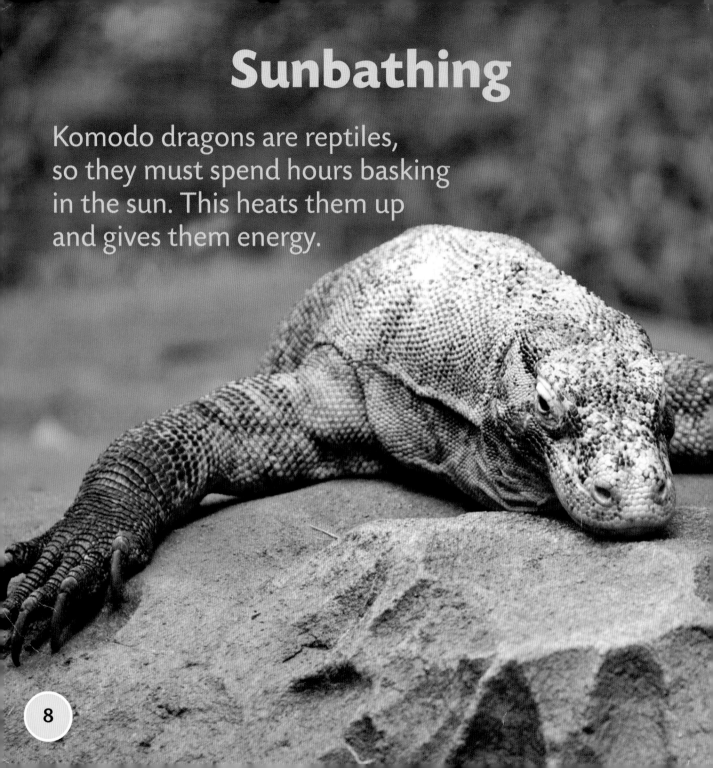

Sunbathing

Komodo dragons are reptiles, so they must spend hours basking in the sun. This heats them up and gives them energy.

When the sun is too hot, they move into the shade or dig holes to shelter in.

Their sharp claws are perfect for digging.

On the Hunt

In the early morning and late afternoon, Komodos are busy tracking down **food**. They do this by smelling—with their tongue!

The long, forked tongue flicks in and out, picking up scents from the air.

Then they wait for prey to come close, watching with beady eyes.

11

Attack!

Komodos *lunge* at prey, **snapping** their fearsome jaws.

They spear small animals
with their jagged teeth
and gulp them down whole.

Rats, birds, eggs, snakes,
monkeys, and lizards
all make tasty snacks.

Greedy Eaters

Komodos also sniff out big, dead
animals and rip off chunks of flesh.
Their jaws open e x t r a - w i d e
to let them take massive mouthfuls.

Komodos are not fussy eaters—they even gulp down horns, hooves, and bones.

When they're full and fat, they rest for several days!

Deadly Bites

The bite of a Komodo dragon contains deadly venom. It is powerful enough to kill animals as big as water buffalo.

They bite the animal's leg, then wait patiently for it to weaken and die.

Lots of Komodos gather around the dead animal and rip it apart.

Fierce Fights

Sometimes male Komodo dragons fight to see who is the **biggest** and best.

First they hiss and open their mouth *wide* to look scary.

Then they stand on their
back legs and wrestle,
swiping each other
with their front legs.
The loser may be killed.

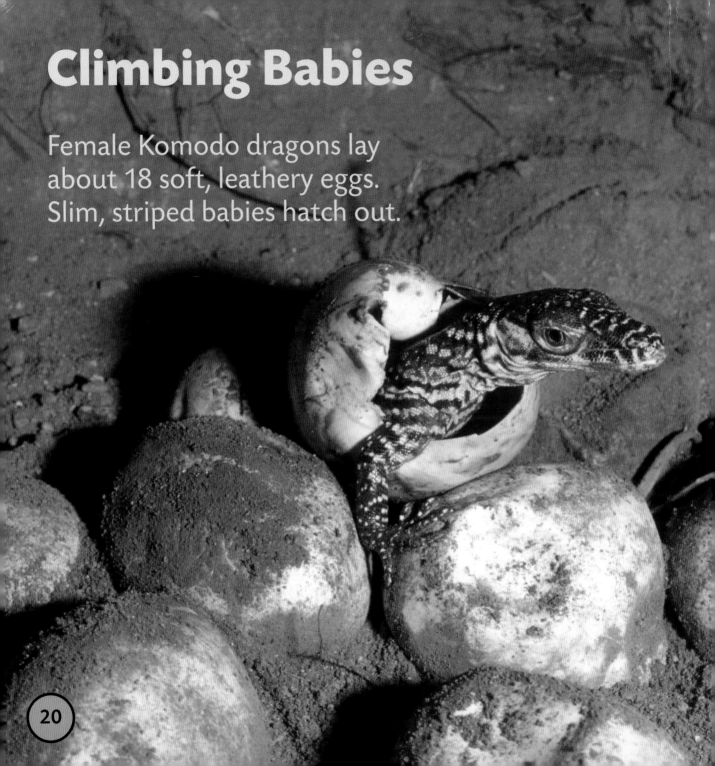

Climbing Babies

Female Komodo dragons lay about 18 soft, leathery eggs. Slim, striped babies hatch out.

Babies may be gobbled up by adult Komodos, so they live in trees for their first year. Adults are too heavy to climb up after them.

They stay safe in the branches, catching insects to eat.

21

BIG Facts

A Komodo can open its jaws wide enough to swallow a whole goat. It takes about 20 minutes to push the animal down into its stomach.

An adult Komodo dragon is longer than you and a friend lying end to end.

A Komodo may swing its huge tail to knock down deer or pigs.

A Komodo could beat you in a short sprint. It holds its body off the ground to run.

23

Useful Words

prey
An animal that is hunted by another animal.

reptile
A scaly animal that lays eggs. Reptiles need the sun to warm their bodies and give them energy. Lizards, crocodiles and snakes are all reptiles.

venom
Poisonous liquid inside a Komodo's mouth that it injects into prey as it bites.

Index

babies 20, 21
basking 8
digging 9
fighting 18, 19
food 4, 10, 13-17, 21, 22
jaws 12, 14, 22
prey 11, 12, 24
scales 5
tail 5, 22
tongue 10
venom 16, 24

Web Link

Visit this web site for great Komodo dragon facts and photos: www.nationalgeographic.com/kids/animals/creaturefeature/komodo-dragon